A special gift for

_____

With love from

_____

Date

_____

This gift edition is comprised of excerpts
from *The Power of a Positive Mom*

Also by Karol Ladd
The Power of a Positive Mom (complete edition)
The Power of a Positive Woman
The Power of a Positive Wife

THe
P wer
OF A
P sitive
M M

HOWARD
PUBLISHING CO.

GIFT EDITION
Karol Ladd

Our purpose at Howard Publishing is to:
- *Increase faith* in the hearts of growing Christians
- *Inspire holiness* in the lives of believers
- *Instill hope* in the hearts of struggling people everywhere
  Because He's coming again!

The Power of a Positive Mom, Gift Edition © 2003 by Karol Ladd
All rights reserved. Printed in the United States of America

Published by Howard Publishing Co., Inc.
3117 North 7th Street, West Monroe, Louisiana 71291-2227

03 04 05 06 07 08 09 10 11 12   10 9 8 7 6 5 4 3 2

Interior design by LinDee Loveland and Stephanie Denney
Cover design by LinDee Loveland

ISBN: 1-58229-291-4

"**Mother**"

describes not only what we do but
also who we are.
From the moment children were
first introduced into our lives,
we became new people—
women with greater purpose,
responsibility, and significance.

1

Life begins with
motherhood.

What could be more invigorating, more life-giving, than a house full of energetic teenagers wanting to be fed, or a handful of toddlers wanting to play hide-and-seek, or a newborn baby wanting to be held?

2

On a large index card, write out your
job description
as a mother.
Include all of your responsibilities
and the name of your "Employer."
Then write out Colossians 3:17 on
the lower portion. Use it
as a constant reminder
of your job significance.

Motherhood transforms
naive, inexperienced
young ladies into wise,
accomplished women
who command
respect.

Mothers possess
a rare form of
wisdom.
We know important information
that others don't—
such as the exact location
of the rest room in every
grocery store in town.

Wonderful Father, thank You for
allowing me to participate in the

glorious
occupation

of motherhood.
Thank You for being the perfect
Parent—and the perfect Role Model.
Bless my family with peace and
safety as we grow to honor You.

6

Being a
positive mom
doesn't mean you have to be a
perfect mom.
A positive mom realizes
that neither circumstances nor
people are perfect.

 7

Don't be discouraged
by your weaknesses;
determine instead
to build on your
strengths.

Prayerfully prepare
your own personal
mission
statement
that reflects what is truly important
to you. Use it as a helpful guide
when you lose your bearings
in the midst of the
whirlwind around you.

9

God has given mothers an
**inexplicable
strength–**
a strength beyond our own strength—
that allows us to tend to
the multiple needs and
cares of our precious charges.

Rejoice

that God is at work
in your life. He created you.
He is developing you.
And He's not finished with you yet!

11

Thank You, God, for not leaving
me alone to try living
life by myself. Thank You for Your
Holy Spirit, who lives in me and
helps me to be a positive, loving,

peaceful,

and joyful person each day.

Help me to be a
positive mom today.

We can make no greater investment
in the lives of our children
than to give them generous doses of

**encouraging
words.**

13

When our young people are
reminded of their God-given value,
they receive deposits of
confidence,
security, and well-being
in their emotional bank accounts.

14

Write out four specific
accolades
for each of your family members
and deliver one of them each week
for the next four weeks.

 15

When we accentuate the

positive

qualities in other people,
the negative qualities
begin to dwindle.

16

Wonderful heavenly Father,
I praise You for Your
omnipotent wisdom
in creation. Help me to accentuate
the positive with my kids.
Help me to be a builder of my family
with the words of my mouth,
speaking praise for the good things
I see in my spouse and children.

We affirm
our kids not because
they are dependent on praise
but because our encouragement
can provide them with the strength
they need to press on
to reach their full potential.

As mothers, our affirming
influence
is like a breeze that firmly sends
the sailboat of our children's lives
across the waters of life. Helping our
children to reach their destination—
to achieve the fullness
of their God-given potential—
is one of the most rewarding
aspects of our job.

To be positive moms,
we need to be
students
of our kids. We must get to know
our children, understand them,
and recognize their
strengths and weaknesses.

Write down
the positive qualities
and attributes you see in your
children in these four key areas of
growth: mental, physical, spiritual,
and social. Spend time with each
child to set realistic goals
for growth in these areas.

21

There is no better stimulus to
motivate
young people toward goodness
than the knowledge that their best
qualities are noticed
and appreciated by Mom.

Our children's
self-worth,
like our own,
must be based on the fact
that God made us
and loves us.

I praise You, Lord,
for having a plan and
a purpose
for each one of us.
You love us, and You know more
about us than we know about
ourselves. Help us to keep our eyes
fixed on You, the author and
finisher of our faith.

A mother's worth is
incalculable.
Few can duplicate our loving touch.
What price tag can be placed on
the sense of warmth and comfort
we bring to our homes?
On the feeling of protection and
safety our children enjoy just
because we are nearby?

25

A simple smile,

offered on a regular basis,

can make a world of difference

in the way our children view
their days, their lives—
and their mothers!

Give everyone you come in
contact with today the gift of

a sincere smile.

Share with your family
how this experience
touched you and others.

Committing to love
and care for our children
as God commands
is the way to a full and
abundant life.

28

Dear wonderful and loving heavenly
Father, I praise You
for the salvation
I have in You. Thank You for
the ability to smile.
Help my children learn
to find joy in life
as they watch my example.

29

You are absolutely

essential

in your home and in the lives
of your kids.
Your job has more
than monetary value;
it has eternal worth!

One of the greatest gifts
we can give our
families
is to stop rushing down the fast lane
and start doing
what matters most.

Decide on a time that would be best
for you to spend in
prayer each day,
and choose a private place to be
alone for that interval.
Write the time and place on your day
planner. Place a Bible, pen, and
prayer journal in your special place
so they're waiting for you
when you get there.

A positive mom
is a praying mom.
Prayer is the most
powerful
resource available to us
in raising our children.

I praise You,
most loving and kind Father, for

hearing my prayers.

It is incredible to think that
the God of the universe would
want to have a conversation with me!
Help me to be a woman of prayer
and a diligent and faithful

prayer warrior for my family.

The ultimate
provider
for the needs of our children
is not us but God.

35

Decorate a shoebox, cut a slit
in the top, and call it your family's
God Box.
Explain to your family that anytime
they're worried about something,
they're to write their concern
on the card and put it in the box
as a reminder that they are
casting their cares on God.

We need to
continually
cast off the worries
we collect and tuck away
in our hearts.

Once we do all that is in our power
as mothers to take care of our kids,
we must leave them
—and our worries about them—
in God's hands.

He is faithful!

I praise You, for You are a wonderful
and caring God.
You know my needs
before I present them to You.
I trust You
with the worries of my life.
I have faith that You are working
all things in my life together for good.

As positive, praying moms,
we need to be
persistent
in our prayers
and never give up.

Through us—
and with His constant,
guiding presence
—God is raising up
the next generation.

 41

Begin today to be a woman of prayer.
Use the ACTS
acrostic (adoration, confession,
thanksgiving, and supplication)
to guide you as you pray.
Ask God to lead you to a trustworthy
friend with whom you can pray
on a regular basis.

We need
wisdom
to survive this job of motherhood—
and the source of all
true wisdom is God.

43

Gracious and loving heavenly
Father, what a joy and

privilege

it is to come to You!
You are the great Provider,
the solid Rock, my faithful Friend.
Thank You for hearing my prayers
and answering in Your time
and in Your way.

44

Contentment

is not based on what you have;
it's based on how you
choose to view life.
It is an issue of the heart.

Hang a wall calendar
in your kitchen.
On the square with today's date,
write one thing that's

good

about this day.
Then, with each passing day,
write a new entry
in the appropriate square.

46

The world may not reward us for our
selfless love
and diligence. It may never give
mothers the credit they are due.
But we can still keep going—
fully assured
that one day we will hear our
heavenly Father say, "Well done."

I praise You, wonderful Father,
for You are able to provide
for all of my needs.
I am confident
that You will never leave me.
Help me to be a positive woman, looking
for the good in every situation that You
allow in my life. Help me to decline the
opportunity to feel sorry for myself.

We can give our children
no greater gift
than a positive,
consistent attitude of
gratitude.
Attitudes are contagious!

Start a
Thanksgiving Journal.

Using a blank notebook,
begin recording your prayers
of thanks to God on a regular basis.
Now and then, reflect on
past prayers to remember
what God has done in your life.

The dinner table is a great place to
begin teaching children about
thankfulness.
As you offer thanks for the meal,
mention several other things
for which you and your family
can be thankful.

Thank You, Father, for Your mercy,
Your forgiveness, and Your loving
care for me. Thank You for my
family—for every good and
not-so-good quality in each member.
Thank You for the

circumstances

in my life this very moment;
help me to see
Your hand at work.

Difficulties in life are
inevitable for all of us.
The question is not
"What are you going through?" but
"What is your perspective and
attitude
through the process?"

53

A positive mom doesn't take away
her children's troubles;
she teaches
them how to look for
the hand of God
in the midst of them.

Make a
Life Map
to illustrate the significant events
in your life—both wonderful and
difficult. To be creative, use photos
and illustrations. Show your Life
Map to your family, sharing how
God has brought positive
things out of the good and bad
times in your life.

Our children need
experiences that
teach them to
cope
without us.

We hurt our children
and block
God's work
when we protect them
from difficulties and
disappointments in life.

Whatever comes your way,
you can be sure that
God is with you
—even at the lowest points.

Oh, Lord,
my comfort
and my strength, thank You
for always being with me.
Thank You for always being there
to hold me up so that although
I may stumble, I will not fall.
Help my family to trust and honor
You through all the circumstances
and challenges in life.

One of the best things
we can do for our children is to
pursue harmony
with our husbands,
doing our part to strengthen
our marriages.

Set a date
and make plans to
enjoy
your spouse.

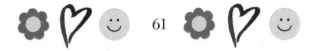

One of the cornerstones
for building a strong family
is a good
marriage.

Wonderful Father in heaven,
I praise You, for You are love.
You love me perfectly and completely!
Fill me with Your
loving-kindness,
especially toward my husband.
Give me the will power and the
creativity to keep the flame strong
in our marriage.

Mothers especially need
one another as
friends.
We need the companionship,
the camaraderie, and the
understanding that
another woman can give.

In a notebook, make three lists:
Acquaintances, Companions, and
Soul Mates. Fill in each list
with names of people in your life.
Pray about working to
deepen
some of those relationships.

Maternal love strengthens us
and helps us
grow
into
**selfless, thoughtful,
and giving**
adults.

Most holy and wonderful Lord,
You are the
Perfect Friend.
You're always there for me.
You meet my every need.
Help me to be a better friend.
Help me to see the new, potential
friends You put in my path each day.

Being a mother broadens our
world-view
and opens our hearts to a deeper
compassion and love for others.
It constantly exposes us to new
challenges and stretches us
to learn new skills.

If you're a young mother,
pray that God will lead you to a
mature woman with whom
you can connect in a
mentoring
relationship. If you're a mature
mother, ask God to give you
opportunities to minister
to less-experienced mothers.

Motherhood is not only
a good use of our
talents
and abilities but
actually increases
and expands them.

Wonderful Father, thank You for the

privilege

of being a mother. Thank You
for the help You give me along
the way. Lead me to mentors who
can share their wisdom and
experiences with me. Show me when it's
my turn to mentor others, and
help me to be a godly example
to those around me.

71

Being an
example
not only takes character;
it takes time.

Write a one-paragraph
description
of the example you want to set
for your family.
Put this paragraph by your prayer
journal and ask God to help you
live out this description.

God has given each of us
the responsibility to train,

nurture,

develop, prepare, and teach
the precious children
He has put in our care.

Is Christ
dwelling in you?
Remember that without Him,
we can do nothing.

Blessed Lord, You are the
perfect example
of righteousness. I love You
and want to live for You
as an example of goodness and
godliness in my home. Thank You
for Your help, Your loving-kindness,
and Your forgiveness.

Start today to
celebrate life
—and watch with joy
as your children
celebrate with you.

Begin a
Family Traditions Journal
using a blank notebook.
Record old and new traditions
for each holiday. Add recipes and other
ideas you collect over the years.
(One day, as a wedding present to your
children, give them a copy so they
have family traditions
to pass on to their children.)

The fun we have and the
memories
we make with our children
will broaden their horizons,
enrich their lives, and prepare them
to pass on special traditions
to their families
for generations to come.

Mighty and awesome God,
thank You for Your loving care for
my family. Help me to be faithful
to pass on traditions
and celebrations that
honor You
and celebrate life.
Help me to live life
abundantly in You.

As parents,
we have been specially
empowered
by God
to pass on His commandments from
generation to generation.

As positive moms, we must take the
initiative to teach
God's principles
to our kids.
Any time is a good time.
Decide what's best for your family,
and then do it!

Purchase a
children's devotional book
that fits the needs of your family.
Prayerfully plan a time
each day when you will
teach your children truths
from God's Word.

83

Memorize Scripture

verses together as a family.
Write the memory verse on a poster. Set
a time limit for memorizing
the verse and offer a reward
for everyone who achieves the goal.

Mighty and
majestic God
of the universe, I praise Your name.
You are powerful, faithful, and just.
Help me to reach the next
generation for You and to glorify You
through everything I do as a mother.

Teach your children
God's value system,
using all the

resources

available. In addition to the Bible,
read books of literature and history.

Visit

an antique shop or used bookstore
and search for old books that tell
stories of great men and women
of faith. Begin reading them
to your children. Talk about
the lessons learned
from the stories.

Teach your children
courage
by studying the lives
of biblical heroes.

Holy and wonderful Lord,
all wisdom and understanding come
from You. You are the creator of all
men and women throughout history.
Help me to pass on great truths—
Your truths—to my children.
Help me to raise
heroes
in the faith within my own family.

Ask God to help you on
a daily basis
to love your family as He loves—
with sincerity, compassion,
and mercy.

90

A mother's love is more than the warm feeling that welled up inside us when we held our babies for the first time. Love requires selflessness, patience, and self-control—and a day-in, day-out commitment to **demonstrating** the sincerity of our love through actions.

Spend some
quiet time
alone, reflecting on God's abundant
love for you. Play soft praise music
in the background
as you read scriptures
that remind you of God's love.

Our children should know
that we are a
safe haven
for them—that we will love them
whether they perform perfectly
or mess up.

Great and holy God,
God of love and mercy,
I praise You for being the

ultimate source

of love. Help me to reflect
that love in my home,
and help my children to learn about
Your love as they see it
reflected in my life.

We show our kids true love
when we set limits and give them
boundaries.
It takes selfless discipline
and strong love to say no
when we know what is best
for our kids.

Discipline should be a
positive
experience. If discipline is handled
with love, it can train our kids
to live effective,
self-controlled, fulfilled lives.

Set aside

a time with each child in which you
talk about God's love and
His guidelines for living.
Help them to understand that when
they disobey or show disrespect or
dishonesty, they're stepping
out of God's plan—
and consequences will follow.

Teach your kids the
Ten
Commandments
(found in Exodus 20).

Our children can rest in the
assurance
of our love when we show them
that we care enough to take time
to lead them and correct them.

Our kids will not always agree
with the discipline we use,
but they will come to
appreciate
it in time.

100

How wonderful You are,
Almighty God! Help me to learn
to discipline by Your example.
Help me to be wise and

discerning

as I train my children.
May my children grow to honor You
with their lives.

A positive woman builds her home
with bricks of support and
encouragement, positive discipline,
and loving forgiveness.
She never forgets the bricks of
daily prayer. And she sets
the Lord Jesus Christ as the
cornerstone
for the whole building.

You are a
builder

—a shaper of your children's world.
You set the attitude and atmosphere
in your home. Yes, you make
mistakes. But you can use
your failures as opportunities
to learn, to grow,
and to become
a better, more positive mom.

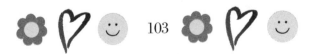

103

Life is its own kind of
classroom,
and we are in the
continuing-education course
called Motherhood 101.

Commit to reading
the most important
instruction book
(the Bible) every day.

We all have regrets as mothers.
We know what we could have
done differently or what could have
been said with a more even temper.
But recognizing that we
all make mistakes, we must
forgive ourselves
and move on.

Our job is to
honor Christ,
not to create perfect kids.
The results of our efforts
are not up to us;
they are up to God.

 107

Wonderful heavenly Father,
You are the King of heaven,
the Alpha and Omega, the Creator of
the universe. How wonderful to
know that You're willing to
help me in my home!
Thank You for helping me
in this incredible
journey
of motherhood.